STONES ARE
THE FIRST TO RISE

David Giannini

DOS MADRES

2025

DOS MADRES PRESS INC.
P.O. Box 294, Loveland, Ohio 45140
www.dosmadres.com   editor@dosmadres.com

Dos Madres is dedicated to the belief that the small press is essential to the vitality of contemporary literature as a carrier of the new voice, as well as the older, sometimes forgotten voices of the past. And in an ever more virtual world, to the creation of fine books pleasing to the eye and hand.

Dos Madres is named in honor of Vera Murphy and Libbie Hughes, the "Dos Madres" whose contributions have made this press possible.

Dos Madres Press, Inc. is an Ohio Not For Profit Corporation and a 501 (c) (3) qualified public charity. Contributions are tax deductible.

Executive Editor: Robert J. Murphy

Illustration & Book Design: Elizabeth H. Murphy
www.illusionstudios.net

Typeset in Adobe Garamond Pro & Beloved sans
ISBN 978-1-962847-16-2
Library of Congress Control Number: 2024949416

ACKNOWLEDGEMENTS

Blueline, A Magazine of the Adirondacks, volume #45:
"Ground Elder (Bishop's Weed)"
"Listening to Music in Fall After Most Birds Fly South."

Misfit Magazine, issue #38, online:
"Gratitude;"
"Interview;
"The Endling;"
"Thinking of Lewis Warsh."

Noon, Journal of the Short Poem, (Japan) Issue #25, online:
"Buddha Gave Us,"
"Extended Koan,"
"Gnomic Miscellany."

Noon, Journal of the Short Poem, (Japan) Issue #26, online:
#4 from "Wellfleet Journal, Cape Cod."

One (Magazine , #30, Jacar Press, online),
"Dark Gray."

Poetry East, #109 (Monet issue, Spring 2024):
"Intuitive Feat: An Assay."

GRATITUDES:

Heartfelt thanks to the following readers of some or all of these poems in manuscript: Pam Bachrach; Stuart Bartow; Joan Digby; Mark Farrington; Elizabeth Giannini; Maxine Giannini; Joseph Hutchinson; Judith (Strauss) Koppel; Jessica Laser; Katie Lehman; Adele Levine; Katt Lissard; Gary Metras; Helen Olshever; Robert Ruchames; Andrew Schelling; Joel Solonche; and Irene Willis.

Thanks to Sean McCusker, artist, who allowed one of his paintings to be reproduced for the cover of this book.

Deepest thanks and love to Elizabeth and Robert Murphy who *are* Dos Madres Press.

Helen Olshever, friend of many decades, I cannot thank enough for her readings of the poems in manuscript, for her invaluable questionings, appreciations, and insights.

I am most grateful to Katie Lehman who read my entire manuscript and provided her excellent and often exuberant comments on it, as well as the blurb for this book.

FOR PAM, ALWAYS

AUTHOR'S NOTE

In *Stones Are the First to Rise*, Buddha, a U.P.S. driver, and an old woman living in hill country shares space and time with stones and peas and war and climate change, plus explorations of childhood and becoming a particular person. Throughout many of his books, Giannini finds himself working with discrete sets of concerns over the course of months or years, concerns that nevertheless cohere as a single envisioning, a book, as the parts of the body cohere to make *body*. Antonio Porchia's well-known words are appropriate here: "I know what I have given you. I don't know what you have received." The book is now in your hands.

TABLE OF CONTENTS

●

●

●

●

●

STONES ARE
THE FIRST TO RISE

". . .I believe the poem is
a sacramental act, pure devotion
to whatever may be revealed only
through the music of intuition. The
dance of the intellect, the dance of the wild
imagination, illuminates what
cannot be otherwise known—a koan,
one's rational and irrational mind
at one."

—Sam Hamill,
from "In Memoriam, Morris Graves."

"The lacerated speech of the big cities."

—Octavio Paz,
The Bow and the Lyre

DARK GRAY

In total darkness, a purplish-red
light-sensitive pigment in retinas
remains abuzz as the optic nerves
make us see dark gray.

In early light, daydreams want us
to go outside and play with bikes
in canyons. In my early years, those
perceptions were my companions:

the dark, the dreams, then objects growing
up, down, around: came more color,
forms, sounds, and a friend or two
with conscience never vacant,

telling that they also envisioned
more than shadows from nascent
nerves and dreams. We still believe
each other again and again. We sense

and believe all the outside world
wants to become more real, enhanced
by dreams, that dark gray is the test
of an optic being intent

on spreading itself further. It wants us
to know what's real skips through
the playground of belief,
swinging and bouncing, facing

bullies and teachers, wind-tossed
rain arriving at the merry-go-round,
the smallest sound a roar to silence,
a cricket's black thunder to the moss.

STONES ARE THE FIRST TO RISE

The stones talk to each other, just as we do. . . .

> — Katsumahtauta (U.S. West Coast tribal elder)
> to anthropologist-linguist Jaime de Angulo

1.

Rain pushing the night down
through melting snow,
                            entering earth
and we felt safe enough
after the storm.
                    We stayed in the ground.

Night could then be turned over

in the morning. . .the dark clods
and puddles with clouds we didn't crush.

Night was coming up through the soil
and vanishing.

Among our kind, that same small stone
turning up, as it did every year,
always rising before us, blind eye
in the night of dirt. Filthy
with what it couldn't see,

as a child without a mirror can't see
its smeared face. Nothing Romantic
or playful. Nothing green. Ancient.

It seemed without knowledge
of what or why it was, surfacing
wet and splotchy, a single syllable: stone.

2.
in late spring

A man began telling
the crushed stones
in the truck-bed
each had the right to remain
silent. Not one listened.
Then they were lifted
higher and higher,
dumped
loudly into their gray language,
their heaped syntax
(no one could decipher)
on the ground. 'One rake
deserves another,' said a worker,
as she and co-worker began
spreading sentences of granite
until the whole story became clear:
the fresh path we could walk
listening to the small nouns,
the ancient ones, turning under our feet,
how they depend, as we all do,
on boundaries, boulders at the edge.

GROVE

Civilization is always rebeginning in the country.—Gertrude Stein

for Gary Metras

How to thwart the clotted thoughts I have
of 'the lacerated speech of the big cities,'
how to forget the rot of the urban, the torment
of trees locked in skyscraper shade, the desperation
of traffic clogged on streets of garbage and smog,
high-rise rooftop bees without sufficient pollen,
the upright and the regular rats running below
through filth in alleys, the constant plague
of the money-markets, and the iPhones
held by suicidal teens everywhere, all
the young who would enclose their sleep,
then close their dreams, forever.

I want to enclose my sleep with oranges,
to leave the world outside of them aside,
to let my heart mix quietly with them
until red and orange yield vermilion dreams—
cinnabar sunrise in ancient times, stone and timber
walls defending forts and cities, often
in countries of sonnets, haiku, ghazals—
now, go to the thriving trees and to the fields:
defend *them* from the cities around.
Stones once grew and trees still reach. Go—make
something more from the planet. Go—write
lines as limbs above concrete and granite!

MAN AND WOLF

For days he was a large man walking on a thin black wire
that disappeared into each night, as an undistinguished
thread vanishes in a dark coat.

He walked on, listening to a wolf, and stared at darkness.
Night was wrapped around and also inside him, as thick wool
even surrounding his heart, but no warmth.

It took the hearth and heat of you, friend, listening
and talking, to unravel his inner cloth. Now, his coat
hangs threadbare in its own bleak closet.

The night is lit like Chanukah or Christmas among lights
and gifts. His feet distort new shoes, the soles too slick
to walk that thread of black wire too long kept.

He strides, and strives to make the wolf sit up and beg,
when all along she has been sniffing him out,
until he is the one begging, without feeling threat.

He tends her. He tries to take care, to caretake
the wolf of poetry, and not be dark-infested
in this heart-clenching world.

Twists & Turns

Sometimes some old madness of the world
reverses, the labyrinth enters the minotaur,
and neither can find its way out. Theseus
doesn't know what to do about the new threat,
it seems made by Plato looking for the Good.

Athena's bird, the owl, goes on through time
and winds up, after Athens, in New York City.
Maps of subway tunnels fade. Your iPhone lights up
in the dark and another light comes to the window
and speaks, but no one can decipher what it says!

There is no answer, no end you can believe beyond
what you imagine, no ending felt in your gut,
only others' and your own notions and time
more and more imaginary, only as real
as the ground-plot you plan at home, full

of Black-eyed Susans, characters of soil, not soul,
uplifting, shifting in wind, sometimes dropping
seed for the next and the next Susan, without need
to know beyond sunlight and each night extending
upright black centers and the orange-yellow whorls.

16 Inversions

The horseshoe waits for the horse.

The base of the fencepost feels the most weather.

There is hidden effort even in stones.

The boulder finally becomes Sisyphus.

Dreams take down their ears before they listen.

Hearing an image means it discovered you.

The orchard in the body picks us.

An old watch confused in a clump of thyme starts running again.

Swoops of swallows restart the wind.

Shells in the garden lick overnight beasts.

The death-appetite for tomatoes is built into the knife.

Our joys attend the anguished yowling beneath all things.

The lamp in memory brightens after it closes.

We remember a river running away from the sea.

The last ripple is also the first one coming ashore.

Death does and doesn't complain when children are born.

THINKING OF LEWIS WARSH

for Katt

As your inner loom weaves it creates the witnessing eye.
The openness of mown fields means none but smallest critters
claw in their mazes—patience connects to Eternity.

Except today, this pastured bull is a hard-boiled detective
held in check by an electric fence. Imported from England,
he knows how to whinge. The enemy's out of range.

I want to see Lewis again, walking with no bull, bearing witness
as he used to, dear man, now dead down in some urban maze
among whatever is among all there. We steeped in our loss of him.

His last book of poetry, *Elixir,* remains the first feast after.
And who could forget, out of his stone-set corpus,
'There are fences around churches to keep the agony from steeping.'

HIVE MIND LATITUDES

Late autumn day—the sounds of worker bees
        entering their hive for winter, after kicking out
all the males, the stingerless drones, to die
        as usual before winter, a few first flying
into our house as their fruitless last ditch shelter
        on windowsills and lintels in sunlight. The encircled
queen keeping to the center of concentric rings
        of workers exchanging outer to inner/inner to outer
bodies to move over honeycomb all winter,
        eating and keeping warm, the protected matriarch
warmest. What does a male bee sense, its yellow
        or white face fallen in the flowerless grass
in a red ripsnorter day of falling maple leaves,
        the splotched ground as if wounded. Exchanges
in the hive continuing in the dark without conflict
        or fragmentation, one ancient modern single mind?
In the human world, our wounds lick us
        until we cross defeat and every answer containing
its own questions, each creating other and further
        questions. What if we all fail in our search for answers?
May we all fail forward into the mastertask of questions,
        while the workers in late autumn, winter ahead,
thrive with their one answer without questions—
        genius is about forgiving being born at all.

LISTENING TO MUSIC IN FALL
AFTER MOST BIRDS FLY SOUTH

for Mickey on her 95th Birthday

Sometimes it seems that voices are tumbling together

in the trees. When we look up through the limbs

nothing but old leaves and abandoned nests,

but the sounds keep moving on top of one another:

something inside wants to let go. Franz Liszt fell

downstairs in a hotel in Weimer. YouTube's playing

his Hungarian Rhapsodies. Leaves beyond the window

hit the ground running. For a moment they hold the music

of dying rapture. Veins of maple leaves are still

visible, and the black-and-white juncos decide to stay

for another winter. Piano keys, but no departure.

INTUITIVE FEAT, AN ASSAY

Especially artists
keep running with one leg
in lifelong childhood
while the other walks to the end
of it. The task
impossible, even grotesque, comical,
but look at Magritte, Moore, Mahler,
or current film, dance, and writings
by all who wind up
buried in their canvas or sharp
or curving free-stand forms,
Hopi pots, Duchamp, digital images,
Hip-Hop, or on paper inside books,
plus graffiti better
than scratch on walls—their early legs
and the later ones are there,
invisible as forever,
and you can still feel their feats,
say the supreme accomplishment
of Monet, the long love
it took all those who desired
the fluid poetry underneath
all art, beyond lilies, all the waves
no one sees, the ones beyond Cause
and Effect, rising in stride
and falling, each
in each other's steps.

THE PAINTER

Hers was the haggard face of the falcon in her painting
dotted with a kind of hoarfrost. She lived high, on a top floor
in the city. Clouds at windows were mayonnaise
mixing with the bottom traffic roar. She said, ' Even the buildings
are not what they seem, is anyone sure deaths from skyscrapers
are not built into their heights?' Her body stiff as a manikin
sometimes fell from misperceived sleights. She said one day
her greater genius appeared below as a distant splat, that
imagination is response but no one reaps more than they can inhabit.
The true artist isn't proud, oh, maybe a little, with a dummy's charm.

You were there to see her art. She caught herself creeping
the floor because she spotted your aplomb. On the day you heard
she'd jumped the railing something rocked you like Emily Dickinson
writing 295 poems in 1863 alone, most of them suddenly cocking
'My Life had stood—a Loaded Gun—.' Alone in 2023, the Emily
who exhibited her art leapt from her balcony. You had acquaintance
with her, emotional remove, sort of like falconry. She and you liked
what flew in her art before she dove. You remember her brow
stayed furrowed from something pulling her deeper down,
pulling her into how and why she didn't need feathers to fly.

On the Gift of an Untitled Collage by John Digby

For Joan Digby

As horns stand up on the deer-goat
the cluster of trees on her back suggests
camel humps above an escarpment,

her long eyelashes and benign eyes
as she steps with the world she transports,
one ear listening to something in an oak.

She floats on white space, sea-waves
splashing up from her belly to the rocks.
Animal of no complaint, the sharp hooves

traveling on air. She may be helping Noah
who has no trees on the god-boat. I call her
deer-goat, and I call her Joan of the ark.

GROUND ELDER (BISHOP'S WEED)

1.

Fall

I gawk at the patch of Bishop's Weed, then
slaughter this *invasive* with a weed-whacker,
but all the roots remain—you thought your
heads should thrive in the air! New shoots will
recharge this plant in spring—I think on. . . .

2.

Winter

roots and bears in torpor.

Birds giving their voices
out of their warmth

as we stiffen outside, and say
rock doesn't know rocks
but we sense their well-being with each other.

3.

After months

a warm day   nothing takes a siesta in the wind.

Able to splay again   clouds open their rehearsals,
day spends itself   polishing its outcome:

the festival of sunset   surely a fiesta
is at hand   as an hour comes to colorful bands.

4.

Now

we're in dusk the Shadow-swallowing-shadows
without torpor, but slow as early spring becoming round
before opening.

Darkness seeps through its hours.
Under our closed eyelids
and because it will not leave us

love happens outside of time

noninvasive

roots routed partially underground.

5.

Our lives

of deep assessments made on the way to the grave,
what would this ant say?

Life's a spell on gravel
to find the good crumbs.

How we hold on, somehow not dead.

What I miss least makes dread
because even it, not I, will live on—

as the Ground Elder starts up again.

SIX ENIGMATIC STAGES

for Joel Solonche

Spring wind can't break
    all stalks or rat nests
so let your hair
    grow wild as brakes.

If life's a jest
    and its polish for coffins
ferret among
    green buds.

To watch one
    leaf unfurling
reflects that spread
    already inside you.

What light can
    inspect our ignorance
respecting it
    as not its own?

Beyond joke or
    coming death
there is green yes
    enough to live this once.

With age 'a sense of
    things more real than things'
moving on-
    to center stage.

SONG: HOLE IN THE BELL

I saw bullet slugs in dew in the early seize
of my old age

        spent shells in a field
        among Charolais

and an old resting bull named Rimbaud
with a copper neck-bell a whistler

        because of a bullet-hole
        in its metal before it rattles

Without breeze
a lying bell won't clap or whistle

        Not all luck withdraws
        without aging

Luck of the draw
is fate's revolver

        I said Don't walk with me
        Rimbaud

Arthur please hold your epitome
at some distance

        Pastured eyes
        have their beads on you. . . .

A Man Invents a Scene from His Past

for Mark Farrington

In a prickly half-circle, a green unbuckled shelterbelt
of hedge. Birds of summer, cheeps in thicket,

the young lovers lying on grass on the other side,
away from the dirt road, and for their first time

slipping off their shoes, removing clothes, thick
together even before the prick and the mound.

We were them once, Suzanne, when trucks kicked up
dirt clouds over the hedge, the house far off,

no one else on the property, and while we were
at it, all our green turned dusty. We were partly

made of disbelief powered by the newness of it all,
laughing, kissing each other through road powder.

We didn't know the end of bliss was just
around the bend, parents returning in a loud car.

You are dead, Suzanne, but remain in me, how
summer and green unzipped us, and the dust.

THATFIELD

where farmers fluff swaths
of new-mown grass in windrows
before baling, white covers enwrapping
giant marshmallows of hay—a simple story,
hard work, personae: the outer aspect
of character merging roles with anima—
you know as well as I do, the best stories break
into poetry, then trudge through plots again,
the baler moving off, men wiping sweat.
I worked alongside men like them,
good men who chewed on stalks
of timothy and never voted Republican,
itchy hay dust on their bodies, some
with hunches to make them flinch
at a grind of gears, remembering
a locked scar once a severe wound.
Covered rolls on the field at dusk,
late birds turning into nests. We may eat
what ate the grass or sip its milk.
Nature, after all, has a vicious aspect:
eat another or die.

Mysteries of the Mirror

for Katie Lehman

The monarch butterfly's orange-&-black means
it's poisonous to birds.

The male goldfinch sees not to taste its own
colors on another creature.

What do you see not to taste? Light's winged reflections
in mirrors with nothing following?

If between your eyelids' flutters you see the wingspan
of poison in a glance

back away from the glass. Also don't faucet. If you swallow
Narcissus will still the tap

but the fountain of youth will keep breaking and entering
with the velocity of a monarch

white drops patching its wings. Monarch never perceives
dusk's shadows knock into each other.

Having no eyelids monarch rests with eyes open in shrubs
or trees at night. Flicker-fire in the flies.

Every mirror has its threshold. Your reversed image transforms
as the mirror peers from its thicket.

When you entered the glass you should've been warned
about the lights and the colors, the savage ones.

ECLIPSE, 2024

As we sit on this lake beach

with the moon between earth and sun

thinking how the Greeks and Mayans

and ancient Asians felt omens and ruined eyes

in the skies of centuries

a heron is standing at the shore's edge

and we say aloud to reassure it and ourselves

Don't worry blackened blue one

Let your genius get the best of you

Wisdom of the body's not just of the brain

and after the great passing

fish will swim the light again.

Replacement Muse

for Joseph Hutchinson

listening

I wake to a cardinal singing in the dark beyond the open window.
Does it exist outside me or inside? Both? Whether it is awake
or not (since some birds practice singing while asleep)
the new muse will stop by later, maybe a hawk in our hemlock.

I fall back to sleep. Clovis spears turn back to unflaked stone.
Mammoths graze safely on open prairies in the wind, heads
nuzzling early grass, sun on blades. No muse, nothing comes
to choose me though fur shines around my ears. I listen.

#

looking

I look at the open geode in my hand. It becomes an abyss
where nothing keeps its points, an abyss with another half,
so I look deeper into that and see it is a well inviting ne'er-do-wells
made mostly of water where humans lose the luck of bones.

Something, like a heart, continues. Whether this drifty shape is real
or not. . .depends on who has eyes and ears. I sleep, and wake
to a cardinal. Oh maybe the new muse an old woman
will stop by later, or just another wolf or coyote on the cliff.

OLD NEIGHBOR

*Preface—there are about 4,000 to 5,000 mail order bride marriages
in the United States every year, and only about 20 percent end in divorce.*

She'd been a mail-order bride from Kentucky
who knew little about farming or 'fucky.'

She worked the apple orchard and had a son
who moved to a trailer with his own bride later on.

She was all the while learning books on her own,
even after her husband was under ground. 'Good bones,'

she said of him. Now old, she lives alone but feels plucky,
this mail-order bride from Kentucky.

OLD NEIGHBOR

1.

When there is constant pain,
smiling is a form of amnesia. Out

of medicated silence and dysplasia,
she gets up to sweep her porch—

dust has no life-wish, but assembles
like life forms. Bristles all groan

in the same way: a bent nail doesn't
roll, a stale roll, a snail. Chairs wobble

and distort—frenetic wicker legs shuffle.
A table is a shifting green sow. Cats

hiss each other behind a wooden beam. Our
neighbor notes through screens the frizzy

heads of chickens in her yard, and recalls
the human skull never fully stops growing,

its bones in aging drift ahead, her skin sags over
eye sockets as the frowns of archways crumble

and she reads Yeats. Lapis lazuli, her ancient
glittering eyes are gay. She lives the pain

she manages, refusing my attempts to assist,
and salvages, for a little while longer, that smile.

2.

She says her face

is always freestyle
when she wakes

then her expressions

weight cheeks
and mouth

without much striving

through her hips
she's ready

to turn

hangdog through stagger
through woe

until her shadow

sits up
and begs.

3.

Her relief in letting go
of the copperhead she found and grasped
on her stone stepway, carrying
then dropping it into woodland, its free
wriggling through wild grass
after its writhing in her tongs first
gripping it on sun-heated stone.

"No serpent senses more
than meets its skin and tongue," she says,
"and maybe the right step's hard to find
when you come up through ground
to feel light and sense the interweavings
of all things and beings, and feel lowly as
'A narrow fellow in the Grass'—
so I say be serious and silly with your fellows
even if you must remove them.
Happy snakes are all alike; every
unhappy snake is unhappy in its own way."

4.

She pets hairs on the back of a bumblebee
gathering nectar
She's done that before with other bees
touching them extra
gently as if swept by a breeze.

At times she feels her hair
in no breeze
stir in open air
and senses the discrete
unknown that touches there.

5.

She said, "You sweat
the world too much, and fret."

She wanted yes,
she wanted back space yet,

she went back not to forget
the old farmers kept

two books at home: they read
Shakespeare and biblical dread.

She said, "How many laborers do you know,
of the two books once winnowed,
have the complete Will in one row?"

She said, "Are there any farmers left alive
who might read or even strive
to read such crucial matter for life?"

6.

One afternoon

I find her sitting on an old car seat on her lawn,

snoozing in a nave of shadow, by a busted rusty chainsaw
near the old yard Madonna once on the half-shell.

Silence is in her chair, as a pillow on a pew seat,

the statue of the Virgin set in dirt, wearing
a metal rosary of once-sharp saw teeth.

Old Neighbor slumps as her dog's ears flick flies.

The bags under the woman's eyes
keep the sag of her sorrows, each big enough

to hold seed from a store of sparrows.

7.

"Don't faze much at wounds
of neighbors," she said, "tread light,

but also don't pretend to graze. Keep heart
even for that lazy sonofabitch, that drunk—

he pretended not to care a whit
for anyone, later shot himself dead.

He took care of himself I guess he did.
In spring someone found one of his guns

in a bear den, right where one
or the other's head would've been,

only lead made him not pretend."

8.

She says a rare guilt
comes to nag:
that she should do more
for the world than poke
her walking stick to help
a porcupine along
safely across road.
She has touched quills
and yanked some
from her dog's muzzle,
every quill a lethal world
working its way
to embed under skin
and migrate toward organs,
a mechanism forced
through what touches it,
barbed dart a
shadow entering blood.

9.

The last time I saw her

She was writing herself a true story
by creating a rhyming inventory:

"More and more toads are more
diminutive than in any borne
year I've known. Fewer and fewer birds,
especially finches and hummingbirds.
More artificial light strikes skies,
world night lights disrupting flight-
migrations. More mosquitoes, fewer bats.
A scarcity of fireflies. That
there are two instead of six
Barred Owls this year. A harsh mix
of winter ice and wind in
trees left a slaughterhouse of limbs.
Also: fatal diseases
in ash, hemlock, and beeches.
Smoke from the burning Earth,
more heat, fewer stars to see. From birth
about 60 percent of life squeezes
and thrives under ground. I sneeze
and think to stay above, for now,
less why than how.
I'll help porcupines.
But there's a type
of quill in the heart's thicket
and I can't get rid of it."

THE ENDLING

An endling is the last known individual of a species or subspecies.
Once the endling dies, the species becomes extinct.

1.

You talk happily to a friend, but sadness holds on
inside both of you. It is the same sadness known

around the world: every angel is trapped in a coffin
of air, lying down on the job. They are still most often

just symbols, without harps, but pry-bars now, just in case
anyone is wondering or praying to open the boxed phase

of oxygen. The angels are bored, occasionally pop out and draw
with lightning. They sketch all the flawed

bozos down below. Well, you get the point. Don't faint, breathe out
and in, slower, go on for as long as forever is, don't look at clouds.

The last angel with the last person will hold
the loudest silence. Most of the dinosaurs: stone.

2.

Filthy windows,
                    sunlight dodging dust
best it can, and no one blames the smear we can't reach.
Dinner on crates,
                    blankets, green splendor in the wraps, talk
opening above shifting chairs:
                              the scatter through glass
a gray jungle. No one can truly hack the battered
world we can't trust,
                    the rust we can't reverse.
The curse:
'The devil runs the world was Adam's discovery.'
In another century,
                    the *Pied Pipers*
led the children onto trains
                              away from the Blitz. Men
and women still come and go
                              none talking of Michelangelo.
Widowers and widows
and bleak windows keep the stage.
                              What devil can it be
whose acid hair descends from sky pillows
and the stones exchange colors?
                              These days
or all days, 'When the attentions change / the jungle
leaps in.'
          and the world's clustered with vicious
screaming, bared teeth, chimp DNA
closest to our own.
                    We are all swinging on long vines.
Double helix. No mirth, no one would choose to be
the *endling*, holding the final human thought and feeling on Earth.

GRATITUDE

Be careful, friend,
                          your skills are approaching
a dead heat between your cast down eye-
lashes of despair and the occasions
of poetry. Chance opportunity can turn
into opera unity, pageantry-and-song,

or say Mongolian horseback falconry
with quivers and shafts on the remembered plain
or stage inside you. Allow all! Allow all heart
against slaughter in Israel, Gaza, Ukraine, the world.

Who doesn't find poetry never truly overcomes despair.

Thanks, at least, for being there and telling
of the rainbow outside your window. I hope
you manage to pull back the sun's arrows,
and let them fly to an unknown country

where one may more than meet the sky.

FAILURE SUITE

Suppose you were an idiot,
and suppose you were a member of Congress;
but I repeat myself.

—Mark Twain

1.

Among throttlebottoms,
muttonheads, jobbernowls,
and other elected dunderheads,

a few will *come to,* come to
clarity, yes, come as prisoners
'come clean' and confess—

so, my humankind, as we go on
for as long as truth has entrails,
with some of you cuffed, chok-

ing on syllables, may we all
come to, 'come clean,' under
the bright lights of failure.

2. *Voting in a Hill-Town*

The porcupine waddles off through duff on the forest floor
and the Speaker of the House leaves Congress for the last time.

The Speaker's head resembles a cartoon turtle, shell: a black spotted suit.
He is really a distort who has discharged his last quills.

Large weasel, the fisher, most deft natural enemy of porcupines,
is already sniffing for prey. We hear a voice near the voting booths say

'Ghosting is not uncommon when it comes to dating app hookups.'
It reminds us of the unregistered, absent but complaining, not voting.

When we exit the spotlights turn on, raccoons and others leave abruptly.
We won't know until later what forest we are in,

who is a weasel, or if the tonsils of a scallywag will be denied vibrato.
The porcupine waddles off through duff on the forest floor. . .

3. *Toward Ukraine*

Those stringed national instruments,
the old banduras, even in war
plucked for their momentary stay

in the clutches of folk
soon shot and bombed,
ripped apart
                    beneath stars.

Already discharged
rifles stick up
in mud,

bones inside clothes,
on the stained hill
weeds—

O ghosts of my kind
can anyone tell
if I'm still a son?

4. *Surgeons at War Borders*

       Here is the heart
       of a Palestinian

Here is the heart
of an Israeli

       What is it these
       hearts teach us

if not you can't
tell them apart.

       Here is the heart
       of a Palestinian

Here is the heart
of an Israeli

       What is it these
       hearts teach us

if not you can't
tell them apart.

       Here is the heart. . .
       Here is the heart. . .

5. *The Saying*

Gaza

The fig not falling
far from the tree, sure,
there is that. Today,

there is this chunk
of concrete split
off from its mother-

lode of a building
after the bombs. There
is a child trying

to lift it out
of the way. It takes
her small heart

pumping hard and
strain of her slim arms—
'Ommi, is this

what it will be like
when I leave you,
will I have to turn

cold and hard and
broken, just to
stay in the world?'

6. *Sun in the Fog*

for Robert Ruchames

The children startled
to see the fogbow, calling it
'a ghost rainbow.'

They so wanted to inhabit it
but first they wanted to know
if the shadow of death was built

into it. What is built into
shadow or fog if not
the light obtaining it.

INTIMATIONS OF RADIANCE, AN ASSAY

The arrival again
of my desire
to understand
heartbreak built in-
to human existence.

Beyond sorrow
there is the beautiful

Portuguese word, *saudade*:
the vague, constant
longing for something
or someone beyond
the horizon of the 'real'—

the longing, the longing. . .

to attain the sense
of something outside
of time—a first animal
or flower, bird, person,
but invisible within
the invisible knot
where they had been
before bodily existence,

without shadows,
without sorrow.

LOVE POEM IN A RESTAURANT

While soy stains chopsticks
we speak of antimatter,
of anti-hydrogen atoms
annihilating harmlessly
in particle accelerators in Switzerland,
and I remember myself as a baby
looking up from my carriage,
laughing at birds in trees. Then
all disappeared. Annihilated?
Memories, too, connect atomically.
Which one is more or less real
than this Mandarin meal
with meandering talk of things
and our mouths packed
with the disappearance act
of ginger string beans? Ha! Will we
remember? No arguments, just tea
taking the sides of its leaves.
What does 'harmlessly' mean
when all affects all? O Universe
your scientists toy and test
with experiments until our hearts
are conceptually reduced
to annihilating bits, spun aspects
in a vacuum tube, while high
soil yields groves of bamboo
for pandas and utensils.
The chill of disbelief is not for soup,
as your atoms, my love, pass a spoon
and touch my atoms as they do,
and ahh, we know our hands
are also us. More tea?

THE GIFT WAS THE OCCASION

The occasion was oak of Asian
descent
a box with carved crickets
on its lid
ones only poets could hear.

Opening
and revealing the box
empty would mean ruin
for the song of the unreal
would lift away.

Best to keep
emptiness inside
sealed
a taut solitude
but no god (we all thought.)

The occasion
was oak of Asian
crickets
chafing in solitude
like poets.

INDIAN MAN WITH ANGINA

In the Katha Upanishad, death needs luck,
say that pachydermic cumulonimbus cloud
and thunder beyond,
                                    as the man steps

from his shop for a moment to look
at clouds, yet fearing ultimate startle,
final flash, his anxiety's
                                    an elephant turning
into lightning.

Inside again, on his back pantry shelf
he finds a forgotten old tomato
desiccated: cap, stem, faded tint,
size of a strawberry—

I know that old man, largethick shopkeeper
hating his own body
holding the damned fruit

and feeling despair with his hand

as if he holds his own heart
in pain from clogged arteries,
his ponderous body

with one hand
dropping
the dried
dead.

BUDDHA GAVE US

an illustrated edition
of Nothing, un-
numbered and unsigned—

Published, read or unread,

out to the Multi-
verse, all our tended
or unattended words
                        there.

For Robert and Elizabeth Murphy
on the twentieth Anniversary of Dos Madres Press

Extended Koan

Walnut. . . window. . . pyramid. . .

things broken make an opening eye
for what is
                    beyond them:

an intelligence

or vexed aspect
of the throng

the nexus
we try to understand

the weird flexes.

WRY ZEN OUTCOME

Eyes closed, basking in the uncontempt
of autumn dawn sun through panes,
you had no choice to be alive
in the first place, but now suppose
choice is yours, and with wry contempt
you choose to restock yourself, imaging
your cells dry as lentils on a pantry shelf,
awaiting water. Or you're just a bag
with invisible means, locus hocus pocus.
You might appear out of a rat instead
of among shelved bulks trying to amount
to a hill of beans, or through a peephole
in an outer wall, showing the sky just
as see-through as before, edges never empty.
It's tempting to give yourself more
shift, lentil uplift in water with a base
of spices, or just to watch a rabbit as the sun
keeps rising higher above the horizon,
raising its all-day roof as a yellow magic hat
with you inside it, then—poof!

A Song of What May Be

Now you can go knock-knock on a tree,
who's there, what's there, is there, are there
catastrophes of character at the borders of sense?

Now you can go, you who are there and not there,
molecules touching as the unseen gray
matter interprets what is, what is believed to be.

Now we are here, kiss me if you want smooth bark
or something deeper, through belief felt
through faces we each believe and feel is another.

Now we may go knock-knock and leave
what is called tree, it and we made largely
of belief, largely with and by whom and what may be.

Meditation & Whiskey

for Helen O. on Her Birthday

Say whiskey in its cask,
say you're like that
fermenting substance
(against the blood-
shed world outside)
so go ahead,
ascribe peace
even to the bunghole
and plug—not
removal from woe
but a reckoning
tooled
oak in the world
adding robust
flavor to what it holds,
the spirit within.

TODAY ON THE MOUNTAIN

All over the where
life is killing me, but I
have to finish it. The joke's

on me. On you. Longanimity's
my name, patience
makes the pace

walking this
downhill
esker

looking back
at that glacier
and ahead to

rejoice in listening
for the boot-
steps of tomorrow. . .

strands of late sunlight
on this precipice
before the abyss,

dusk a gray wand
a sign
This orifice is temporarily closed

I can't see to hike
back down the rocky
now my heart's

a rescue beam
the path
the mountain inside me.

GNOMIC MISCELLANY

for Adele Levine

Anonymous Bosc

To learn from a bowl of handsome pears! First, all pears are *the* pear—proceed.

Silt-Sand-Clay

Tongue under the brook is also the brook, but its words are above it.

February

Sequestered long in maple all the sap's patience at the tap, tested.

Deaf Child in the Steeple

Wanting the church bell to hear silence, she puts its rope end to her ear.

Span

Each syllable crossing a bridge   over undertows beneath each word.

Fertile

After hard rain the field lifts, we lag behind the genius of the pea.

Wellfleet Journal, Cape Cod

for Pam

1. Far Away Here

Whatever shapes our seeing has a shape
we can't see. "A brain thing" vagary
won't do. Say an old woman on an old pier
looked beyond waves to the horizon.
Her daughter now stands as her mother
once stood with her and pointed.

It is that her mother understood
her daughter would recall how they stood.
That *then* had a shape brought forward
into now. That shape is part of why and how
that daughter now on the same pier
takes her own daughter's small hand at the end
of day, index fingers of their other hands
pointing to the horizon they will take away.

2. Sea Bay Restaurant

We didn't begin
or end wonder
but ended wondering
where the poetry
of wonder began

then conversation turned
and we pungled up for pie
after fish steak out
of our carnivorous
relation to animals

as we looked out
at the angler in her little
boat rocking from ripples
from an unknown source
across the bay

and still on course
we imagined her a poet
sensing words sensing her
before wondering
why she rocks in rhythm

and what might come
to succeed her silence
and become more
than that fish now
yanked out flopping.

3. Watermeal

We may never catch a glimpse of the world's smallest flower rafting in marshes, slow ponds, and lakes, clustered (thousands could fit inside a screw-on water bottle cap,) producing the world's tiniest fruit that some Asian people cultivate as food. Having no roots, Watermeal floats, often asexually reproducing daughter plants, two every three days. It often chokes out other aquatic life; or if kept in check it can serve to clean waterways of excess nutrients and provide nourishment for fish, fowl, and Bashō's

old pond

frog leaping

plop!

4. Notes on the Way to a Beach

That marsh
still holds
the time
we held.

_____

Backroad forest
of dead bony pitch pine
and one wren
singing on a skeleton.

_____

Raccoon family
also crossing the bike path
heading toward the beach.

_____

Fern wings bob in rain,
spider tightens her rigging,
the green ship sails on.

_____

Finally sun   burning striations
of ocean fog   strewn as bled veins

as the ocean   sounds in our blood
a red dog   in the waves.

5. Women Surfing

Everyone
        scanning waves
                for sharks
while that man
        without arms
                seated in sand
also watches
        the three
                young surfers
shiny in
        wetsuits
                black as
dolphin backs
        slipping down
                to racing shore-
line stones
        a solitary seal
                in the waves
watching
        them and
                the man
who would
        if only
                he could
embrace
        each
                one.

6. Partially Remembered Seaside Nightmare

A voice: *Disregard the fin and you'll soon disappear—*

before I was in bits and pieces I caught one of my nostrils
alternately working harder than the other again, naturally,
as I was ably human, unable to disregard scents. . .

think to reshape the inevitable. . .

in order to keep it at a solving distance,
knowing I'm the chum it had come to devour,
my never-released scream
held on the tongue of chaos, then its teeth. . .

before that, you were a kid. . .

brought a jar to the ocean, took ounces of wave
home to a windowsill. Waited
for the moon. Moonlight at the jar
but in the water: no wave. Unscrewed the cap.
Still nothing moved. Recapped.
It seemed a solution against a foreign power
in space. I didn't know which way to move.
My legs stood, but stride stayed inside them. . .

unanswered questions, the best kind. . .

then the sea became an answer to the wind
rushing over it in question mark curl of current
while outer space remained
the unchanging occasion of itself
with the moon
in it, all right,

what the hell. . . .

7. The Moon as Puppeteer

More bleak *Breaking News* screams
online these days, so some people stay
indoors, alone, dream of an island where
even stiff introverts may dance.

At the island's *Dance of Marionettes*
all the marionettes vanished,
only their strings were left
tugging each other and tussling

until some were strung like fishing nets
and felt they were married.
A few went to catch fish. Caught
fish seemed like marionettes to those

fraught in a married net. Unmarried
strings felt betrayed and left. They
wondered if they were real and truthful,
so they began weighing themselves

on the scales of authenticity. A few
investigated String Theory. Others just
looked at waves, those eyelids of the sea,
those liquid marionettes, no strings attached.

8. What the Waves Said

This ocean spirit is /
                 also your own /
always broken /
              unbroken /
hence these waves /
               continuous /
discontinuous /
             another form /
of paradox /
           formless /
form of the whole /
               pulling its shores /
under /
       while you hear /
in the crashing /
             what's shattered /
is also whole /
           as you are /
soon pulled /
         ahead /
back.

9. Salt Song

When the crack of dawn holds both
sun line and thunder, the animating spirit
of all, restless as sea salt,

when the crack of dawn holds both
your smile and under,
I come to you, taste salt, and enter.

10. Night Storm at Home
      After Dolphin-and-Whale-Watching at Sea

All lights go out. In our pitch-black house
our eyes adjust and perceive all as dark gray,
the same shade seen by most humans in lack
of light, scientists say. There must be some

source coming from inside the skull,
as an old lantern in the ship captain's helm,
or lit particles of a self-organizing whole
seeking how to move through the brewing dark

paths in our house for dolphins, humpbacks, stone
corridors where Macbeth rages before candle flames
and Lennox says, 'Some say the Earth
Was feverous and did shake.' We can't take the idea

of too many witches or this thunderstorm where
that old druid tree struck by lightning is far enough away
but we feel its thunderkin screams through our skin
and a vague voice inside an old light gray as charcoal,

and the humpbacks, how much they must see
and hear in their darkness, calling to each other
as the new-born calf arrives, and five hundred
white-sided dolphins leap the waves.

Coming To, an Assay

*An offshoot and kinship in part indebted
to Laura (Riding) Jackson's* The Telling.

We wake. We come to
our first words gently,
ma-ma glows in the mother's ear.

Still inside her we felt no god
but the uncaused original Whole
with its need to project itself myriad,

then test the underlying sorrow
of all things and beings
longing to be as Whole was

before its original acrobatic splat,
the Big Bang, the Multiverse, the imp
beings plumping out

without sound until pat,
then coming to
invent language that will put

the Whole back together again,
that it will know itself true
when all things tell of the Whole.

Our mind-body begins with slitherings,
then recognition
and gratitude toward others,

some say it's all up from there
as *ma-ma* glows in yet another
mother's ear.

BLINKING ALL DAY

Your unborn infant's stardust still
assembling, even now there are words coming toward you
with the velocity of a heartbeat—

what will unfold is already between you:
'the small pink orifice mimicking its mother's newborn cry,'
the beginning of steps from and of another speck

of the infinite with its underlying wail, its yearning
to be in the brilliant twinkling chaos of being at all—
dear child, blinking, the human universe blinks all day.

NIGHT OWL

Every night makes its point
or no point. What's the point
if not what your eyes and ears

and all your senses make
from being as you are
the sum of you finding meaning.

Your child cries out from her dark
because something she can't see
scratches in a wall beside her.

What if direct connection is over
at night, or just maverick
as a mouse gnawing wood in

a closet or stover in a field
and you're the owl suddenly
at it. A tall door opens a taller view,

a lit bulb in the hall all night,
the shadows conquered
and when the closet's illumined

the sounds in the wall stop—
you comfort the child with light,
touch, and your tender voice.

She will sleep, an owl-in-daylight,
She will sleep with an inner light too,
like the child inside you.

Eidolon, Palm Sunday

Below a kettle of hawks riding thermals
sat a charm of finches on branches

or all these were diurnal phantoms
wanted, waited for, apparitions

of flight and perch to remember
outside that church where you sat, a kid

sensing inside yourself an elegant palm
leaf bowing and turning into a day-

dream searching for the flight
and voice of your abandoning mother.

Unjarring

The boy learned to call a fly *mother*
after his real mother abandoned him. Father
and other relatives were more than real enough
and offered accumulating pity best

set aside. It was a peach tree and fireflies
showed him how to be a boy steering
around globes at dusk, Magellan and his circum-
navigating crew with lanterns at night.

So also the natural world raised him as he raised
himself from feeling he was a captured one.
That was a way he felt his mind being
made as it was growing and making him freer.

He learned to call the sky *mother,*
no abandonment by it, ever, and savored
sapid fruit after the fire synced with flies
was caught, then freed from a closed jar.

THE ENIGMA

mother and daughter. . .

Well, dear, no one usually notices the missteps of the Enigma, how we coincidentally came to be people, then people with people, freaks that keep thinking there is something more to mean.

You mean, like Christmas has no place to go, mommy, except the same hole, the one that waits all year, right? You told me we all have to fill our own hole each year, *every* year. Now, my hole and your hole has grandma dead inside, sorta like *twice*, yeah, I miss her, but there's also cheers and cheese and fish and nuts and the same stupid arguments around the table, same carols too, for each hole, and fresh cookies and drinks to fill us up! And thanks again, mommy, for Whack-a-Mole, I get it: we all have to pop up again even when there's nowhere else to go, except the next hole, and no one notices the dumb missteps of a mole.

U.P.S.

grandfather. . .

When the young woman, Skye, knocks at the door,
you become the old face inside the package she carries.
Yell through and thank her and unseal from within!

Now the woman's face is inside the open package with you.
Looking up, you each notice some trees outside, fallen
because of the wind, but others have new leaves. Some dust.

There are two leaves in the unpacked box, one
with an old face, one still unfurling, somehow each alone,
but how can that be? An unsealed world breathes.

The forest keeps swaying over the wounded briars
and now the windows all have the same kenspeckle truck
brown as a trunk bumping down the lumpy dirt road.

HOUSE OF THE BODY

father...

The human body is full of dark beams.
Only one light enters
and remains for the rest of each life—

it won't leave our fleshly house easily.

The house of the body stands its seasons
and sometimes its shadow cracks from the least wind
and then comes back together again—in Fall

'How the sick leaves reel down in throngs!'

The winter of the body further darkens its beams.
Leafless branches invite the house outside.
The light-soul has a shadow cast by the body—

one reason we keep an eye out for sun.

A PLEA

for L.

Dark moods are often shadows of thought
passing through the body, unrecognized in transport,
sometimes arriving as night snow is, as they say, *driven*,

winter
    already blowing
        and drifting
            inside your cave.

Please be tender with your truth. It is already shoveling its own path
inside you, clearing the way to share your solitude.

Matisse, when he could no longer hold a paintbrush, asked
that one be tied into his hand.
                        Didn't Mozart understand
the future on his deathbed, the white sheets with the dark ink
of his *Requiem* still drying?

SMALL WORRIES ALL NIGHT

Small tufts of wool try to leave the sweater
but they're still stuck in the greater pattern.

Worrisome thoughts are like that! They each
would go back to the barn before the shearing.

They would rather go out to the hill and nibble.
My sleeplessness has a sheepish aspect that way.

In the morning I put on the sweater and ignore
the shears. Let the sheep graze. Later, I'll sleep.

STAGES OF CONSTRUCTION

Every dream is at first naked
someone under a dark sheet
the body is dream's clothing

I am naked and clothed at once
as the construction starts
from the earth of my body

assembling toward stars
the scaffolding to be
in front of no building

just my own mind reaching up
fitting steel in front of nothing
before space

birds on the rails
those little dinosaurs
singing under sun

and what if trembling
in my own last evening
I will look up and see crows

as pieces of night flying
toward some destructed end
of all perches

and find myself then in shadow
under slow or swift wings
turning back. . .

Thinking Back Down Inside Me,

Sketch-and-Assessment

Many things oval and round still have their rolls here,
childhood's painted eggs and marbles. Targets and goals.

There is still the sense of a bull's-eye approaching at great speed
to surround the arrow, then the bow, then me.

Some old nights and days still gather and settle their disputes
and pain with multiple cries, voices of mourning doves.

Too many rectangles took over: ideas and 'facts'
settled in textbooks forced under my eyes like dyed ice-blocks—

'the drying and freezing process which goes by the name
of education.' The gaslighting. The taunts.

A green circle found to betray time by living outside of it
is what I wanted, without knowing why. Poetry sighed.

Learning how to grasp something whole
without enumerating its parts: intuition. It has no time.

Coming to grips with the nature of paradox,
I have as many contradictions as the next man.

It's sometimes difficult to move from shells and linear planes.
How my life's accrued. . .to be continued. . .contained. . .or just left

as my whisper leaves my breath on a windowpane in a cold room,
no one and nothing listening outside. No witness.

Interview

Q: Why have you written so many poems about poetry?

A: I didn't write them; they wrote me. I'm not being flip, that's the initial process or sense, sort of like this interview. I sense images and words sensing me, then we proceed.

Q: I'm not sure what you mean, Automatic Writing?

A: No. Put it this way: Say I pick up a twig. Pretty soon the Boss arrives, sees me with the twig, and demands that I make a board out of it.

Q: How can you do that? That's not possible.

A: Imagine.

Q: And then?

A: The twig starts growing and becomes flat, lengthening and widening, looking very rough-sawn, but somewhat handsome in its lines.

Q: What then?

A: Soon the Boss returns and commands me to make many boards, of different sizes, milled and sanded, until I have enough to build a house.

Q: Yes, and. . .?

A: I build a house—a good shack or a place of multiple rooms and storeys.

Q: May I see one?

A: You're in one now with me. It's only partly finished, it still has drafts.
We can be quiet and just listen.

Q: To what?

A: If you have an ear for it, there are many sounds like many nails being hammered together into a larger structure, but each nail has a voice, like a bird brought forward through the words of our ancestors, but freshened. They are sometimes loud, other times not so. Pretty soon many bits of the universe come to knock, enter, and participate, like you.

Q: Why do you build so many houses?
A: I couldn't live anywhere else.

Q: Last question. Who is the Boss?
A: Beats me.

NOTES

P.4: In "Grove," line #2, the quote is from Octavio Paz, book *The Bow and the Lyre*.

P.41: In "The Endling", #2, the first quotation is from "Oxford" by Fanny Howe. The second quotation is from Charles Olson's "The Kingfishers."

P.74: Re: #8 in "Wellfleet Journal, Cape Cod", during our boat tour there were suddenly and literally 500 white-striped dolphins around the boat, verified by the Captain of the boat and a marine naturalist onboard.

P.80: This line in the poem, "Blinking All Day," 'the small pink orifice mimicking its mother's newborn cry,' is by Katie Lehman; my thanks to her.

P.86: Re: "House of the Body," the quotation is from Thomas Hardy's poem, "During Wind and Rain."

ABOUT THE AUTHOR

DAVID GIANNINI's most
recent full-length collections
of poetry include *Already Long
Ago*; *The Dawn of Nothing
Important*; *In a Moment We
May Be Strangely Blended*;
Mahap; *The Future Only Rattles
When You Pick It Up*; *and Faces
Somewhere Wild*; He was twice
nominated for the Pulitzer

Prize and The National Book Award. *Porous Borders,* a book
of prosepoems, was published by Spuyten Duyvil Press in
2017.) Numerous chapbooks of his poems and prosepoems
have been published by a variety of small presses through
the years, and his poetry has been published in national
and international magazines and anthologies. He received
Massachusetts Artists Fellowship Awards; The Osa and Lee
Mays Award For Poetry; an award for prosepoetry from the
University of Florida; a Finalist Award from the Naugatuck
Review, and a Finalist Award for the James Hearst Poetry
Prize of The North American Poetry Review in 2021. He
has been a gravedigger; beekeeper; taught at Williams
College, The University of Massachusetts, and Berkshire
Community College, and he taught preschoolers and high
school students, among others. Giannini was the Lead
Rehabilitation Counselor for *Compass Center,* which he co-
founded as the first rehabilitation clubhouse for severely
and chronically mentally ill adults in the northwest corner
of Connecticut. www.davidgiannini.com

Photo by Judith Strauss Koppel

www.ingramcontent.com/pod-product-compliance
Lightning Source LLC
Chambersburg PA
CBHW050857150626
46549CB00013B/2591